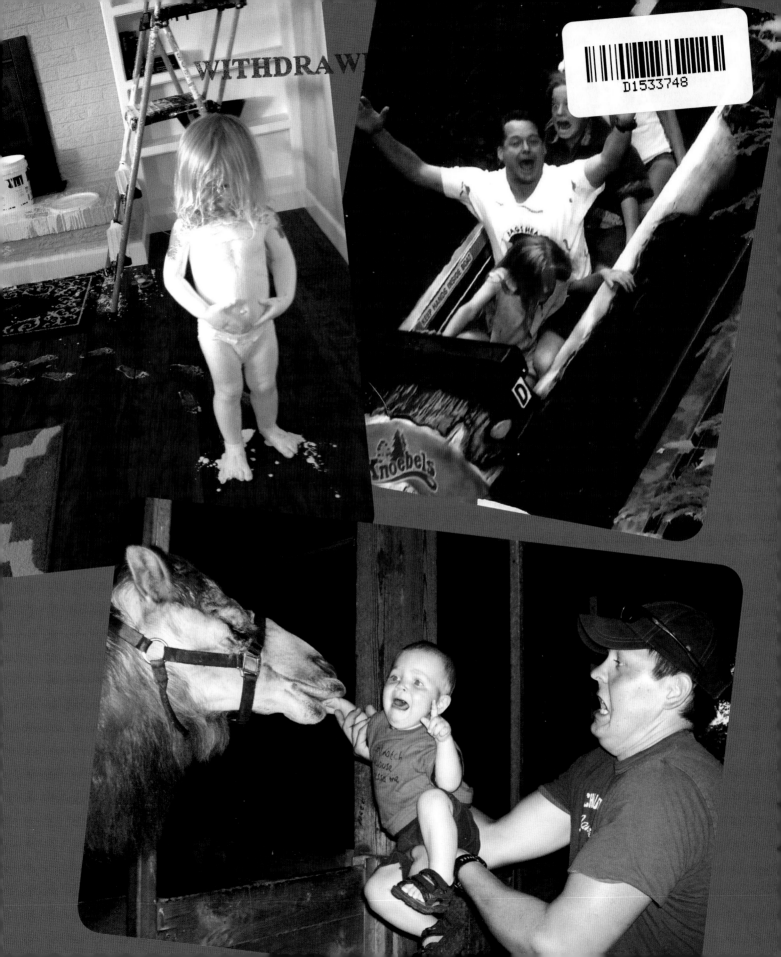

EVERYTHING IS AWKWARD

MIKE BENDER &
DOUG CHERNACK

CROWN BOOKS FOR YOUNG READERS
NEW YORK

To Kai, Soe, Ravi and Violet—
Embrace the Awkwardness.

Copyright © 2016 by Awkward Family, LLC
All rights reserved. Published in the United States by Crown Books for Young Readers,
an imprint of Random House Children's Books, a division of Penguin Random House LLC, New York.
Crown and the colophon are registered trademarks of Penguin Random House LLC.

Visit us on the Web! randomhousekids.com
Educators and librarians, for a variety of teaching tools, visit us at RHTeachersLibrarians.com

Library of Congress Cataloging-in-Publication Data is available upon request.
ISBN 978-0-399-54984-7 (trade) — ISBN 978-399-54985-4 (lib. bdg.) — ISBN 978-0-399-54986-1 (ebook)

MANUFACTURED IN CHINA 10 9 8 7 6 5 4 3 2 1 First Edition

AWKWARD

It's kind of a silly word.
But all it really means is that
everything isn't always perfect.

Like eating.
Sometimes the food goes in your mouth.

Sometimes it ends up everywhere else. And that's PRETTY AWKWARD.

Sleeping can be awkward too.
You might fall asleep in your bed....

Or you might
fall asleep . . . HERE.

Scratching your nose isn't
really that awkward.

Picking your nose is DEFINITELY AWKWARD.

You might want to sit on the potty...

But end up in the potty. Which is **SUPER AWKWARD!**

It's fun to take a bubble bath.

It's **AWKWARD** to take a bubble bath**ROOM**.

Starting the slide on your bottom. Normal.

Ending on your face. AWKWARD.

Riding a bike can be easy.

Falling off can be—wait, what's that word again? Oh, yeah. AWKWARD.

Some days, you might catch a fish.

Other days, you'll catch yourself. Ouch, **AWKWARD.**

Vacation can be full of smiles.

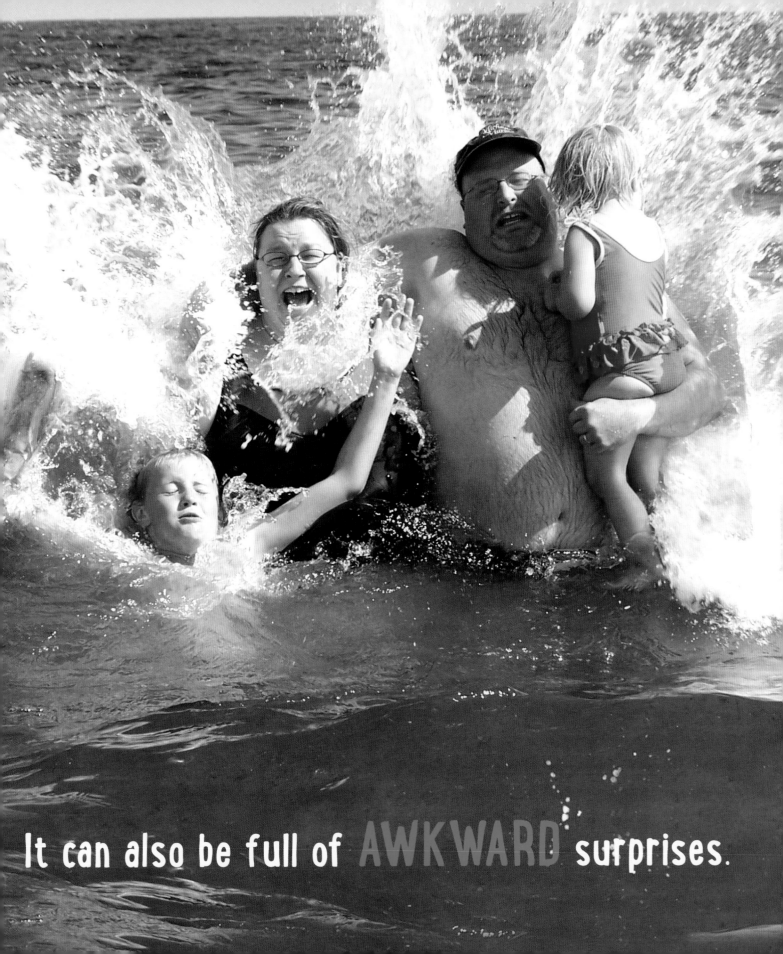

It can also be full of AWKWARD surprises.

And it's not just
everything that's
AWKWARD.

EVERYONE is
AWKWARD
too!

Like your parents.

So AWKWARD.

Your siblings.

Even dogs. But you're probably wondering
what's awkward about dogs.

They
LICK us.

SNIFF us.

And POOP
everywhere!

As you can see, everything
and everyone is AWKWARD.
But you know what?

AWKWARD is kind of fun.
And perfect is . . . well,
kind of boring.

So you don't have
to be perfect.

You just have
to be **YOU.**

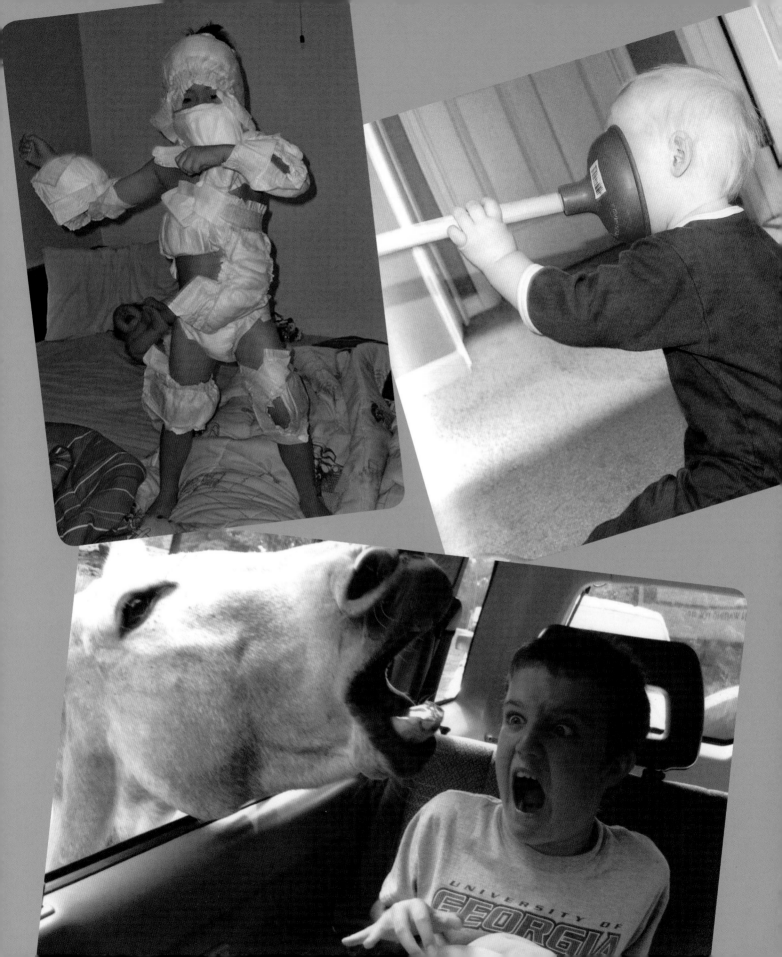

Even if that means you're a little **AWKWARD** sometimes.